What did grandpa and you like doing the most together?

What was the nickname grandpa gave to you?

What does grandpa's voice sound like?

What was grandpa's favourite snack to eat?

Are you still doing all the things grandpa taught you to do?

What did you wish you could have said to grandpa more often when he was alive?

What gift did you give to grandpa that he was really happy to receive?

What did grandpa and you like to do during the summer season?

How have your friends supported you after grandpa's death?

What did grandpa and you like to do during the winter season?

What did grandpa and you like to do during the fall season?

How are things been with grandma since grandpa is no longer around?

What did grandpa say he liked the most about you?

What did grandpa say you should do when he died?

If you could change something about how you said goodbye to grandpa what would it be?

Do you remember grandpa's favourite hobby?

What type of drink did he like the most?

What did grandpa do a lot that made you laugh?

What did grandpa say about the afterlife?

Did grandpa like any sport and if he did, was he good at it?

Do you remember what favourite clothing grandpa liked to wear?

Do you remember what favourite shoe grandpa liked to wear?

What funny story did grandpa tell you that made you happy?

What would you like to tell grandpa that you didn't get a chance to say to him?

What did you promise grandpa you will continue to do when he died?

What music did grandpa liked to listen to the most?

What would you like grandpa to know about in the afterlife that you are proud of doing now?

Did you have a nickname for grandpa?

What favourite snack did grandpa get or made for you?

Have you been feeling differently without grandpa being around?

Write down grandpa's favourite food?

How did you feel when grandpa was getting buried?

What do you talk to dad or grandma about after grandpa's death?

When grandpa was ill at the hospital or at home, how did it make you feel?

What did grandpa and you like to do during the spring season?

What do you talk to mom about after grandpa's death?

How are things been with your siblings since grandpa is no longer around?

Write down your favourite memory of grandpa?

What did people say they liked the most about grandpa?

How do you feel about grandpa not being around anymore?

Made in the USA
Monee, IL
27 March 2021